Reclaimed Quilts

Sew Modern Clothing & Accessories from Vintage Textiles

Kathleen McVeigh & Dale Donaldson

stashBOOKS.

an imprint of C&T Publishing

Text, photography, and instructional artwork copyright © 2024 by Kathleen McVeigh and Dale Donaldson

Pattern artwork copyright © 2024 by C&T Publishing, Inc.

Publisher: Amy Barrett-Daffin

Creative Director: Gailen Runge

Senior Editor: Roxane Cerda

Editor: Madison Moore

Technical Editor: Debbie Rodgers

Production Coordinator: Zinnia Heinzmann

Illustrators: Dale Donaldson, Jennifer Hastings

Photography Coordinator: Rachel Ackley

Front cover photography by Kathleen McVeigh and Dale Donaldson

Photography by Kathleen McVeigh and Dale Donaldson, unless otherwise noted

Published by Stash Books, an imprint of C&T Publishing, Inc., P.O. Box 1456, Lafayette, CA 94549

Attention Teachers: C&T Publishing, Inc., encourages the use of our books as texts for teaching. You can find lesson plans for many of our titles at ctpub.com or contact us at ctinfo@ctpub.com.

We take great care to ensure that the information included in our products is accurate and presented in good faith, but no warranty is provided, nor are results guaranteed. Having no control over the choices of materials or procedures used, neither the author nor C&T Publishing, Inc., shall have any liability to any person or entity with respect to any loss or damage caused directly or indirectly by the information contained in this book. For your convenience, we post an up-to-date listing of corrections on our website (ctpub.com). If a correction is not already noted, please contact our customer service department at ctinfo@ctpub.com or P.O. Box 1456, Lafayette, CA 94549.

Trademark (™) and registered trademark (®) names are used throughout this book. Rather than use the symbols with every occurrence of a trademark or registered trademark name, we are using the names only in the editorial fashion and to the benefit of the owner, with no intention of infringement.

Library of Congress Cataloging-in-Publication Data

Names: McVeigh, Kathleen, 1987- author. | Donaldson, Dale, 1983- author.

Title: Reclaimed quilts, sew modern clothing & accessories from vintage textiles / Kathleen McVeigh, Dale Donaldson.

Description: Lafayette, CA : Stash Books, an imprint of C&T Publishing, [2024] | Summary: "Build a one-of-a-kind quilted wardrobe with vintage quilts! Join Kat and Dale in exploring the world of one-of-kind, work-of-art garments and building a stunning wardrobe. Ten projects are included inside that span from simple accessories, like totes and small bags, to full outfits, including jackets, and dresses"-- Provided by publisher.

Identifiers: LCCN 2023053893 | ISBN 9781644033623 (trade paperback) | ISBN 9781644033630 (ebook)

Subjects: LCSH: Quilting--Patterns.

Classification: LCC TT835 .M4783 2024 | DDC 746.46/041--dc23/eng/20240105

LC record available at https://lccn.loc.gov/2023053893

Printed in China

10 9 8 7 6 5 4 3 2 1

DEDICATION

In loving memory to Elsie Anthony and Donna Donaldson, the original quilters of our family. Their creativity and love for sewing are the spark behind this book.

ACKNOWLEDGMENTS

We would like to thank our friends and family for their unending support of us in starting this business; they have been our cheerleaders, editors, critics, customers, models, prop stylists, photo assistants, and so much more. We would not be here today writing this book without them.

Special thanks to Carey Nershi and her cat Topo for helping with nearly every single aspect of this book project. Thank you to Andrea Brito-Nuńez, Avery Rosenbloom, and Julian Hackney for bringing our clothes to life, and to Evan Nershi for his assistance in running our shoot. Thank you to Dre Falzarano and Cherie Marshall for the use of their beautiful backyard, and to Barge Canal for letting us photograph inside their amazing antique store.

CONTENTS

UPCYCLED CLOTHING:
SUSTAINABILITY AND PRESERVING HISTORY

As we continue to learn more about the effect we humans have on climate, more and more people are looking for ways to reduce their environmental impact. Choosing to incorporate sustainable fashion into your wardrobe and support clothing companies in the fashion industry that are producing clothing sustainably has become a powerful option. Perhaps you're wondering what makes clothing or a brand *sustainable*.

In this book, we'll explore how the concept of sustainability applies to fashion through incorporating vintage materials into our contemporary sewing practice. We'll also explore how working with these textiles honors the history of the makers who came before us.

What Is Sustainability?

At its core, sustainability is about meeting the needs of the present without compromising the ability of future generations to meet their own needs. It means developing practices that don't deplete finite resources, damage the environment, or threaten the future of the industry or Earth at large. In the context of fashion, this means creating clothing and accessories that are durable, long-lasting, and made with materials and processes that have a minimal impact on the environment.

SUSTAINABILITY IN FASHION

Unfortunately, the fashion industry has historically been one of the least sustainable industries in the world, and a huge part of this can be attributed to fast fashion.

Fast fashion refers to the rapid production and mass marketing of trendy clothing at low prices in response to the latest fashion trends. This model emphasizes quick turnover, allowing fashion brands to change their collections quickly and constantly. Ever notice how that surprisingly affordable piece of clothing that was all the rage a few months ago has already gone out of style? Or how even if you have a full wardrobe, you're left wanting the "latest thing"? That's no coincidence. Fast-fashion brands thrive on marketing to consumers in a way that leaves them feeling like they need more.

This type of clothing production is a cause for extreme environmental concern, in that brands produce more than they will sell, since the item is only fashionable for a few months, and the result of that is excessive waste and landfills filling up with millions of tons of discarded clothing each year. There are ethical concerns as well. When an item's price tag is low, the cost to produce it is even lower. When the goal is to produce something as cheaply as possible, there are often severely underpaid workers, laboring in extremely hazardous conditions.

Ernest Rose

Kitty Badhands Sustainability Practices

 Kitty Badhands, the sustainable fashion brand we created, makes sustainability a core part of its practice. We use vintage and sustainable materials—fabrics made using natural materials and produced in a manner that has a low impact on the environment—in our work. We create pieces that are designed to last. We also believe in transparency and ethical production practices, which means we know where our materials come from and how they were produced. By creating the projects in this book with vintage and upcycled materials, you're doing the same—creating pieces designed to last with sustainable materials.

Preserving History

Using vintage materials, particularly handmade materials like quilts, in your sewing projects is not only sustainable, but also a way to honor the history of the makers who came before us. Vintage clothing and textiles are often imbued with a sense of nostalgia and history, and incorporating these materials into your work can create a connection to the past that is both personal and meaningful. We began our clothing-making journey by using vintage quilts to create coats. It was through this process that we came to realize that we were not only using materials that already exist on the planet (instead of creating a need for more fabric production), but also breathing new life into textiles made by amazingly talented artists and makers from the past. Every artist deserves to be remembered for their work, and by upcycling these art pieces instead of leaving them to rot or be thrown away, we're providing new ways for folks to rediscover the beauty of quilting in a modern context.

Members of the women's club making a quilt. Granger Homesteads, Iowa. Photo by John Vachon

Creating modern clothing from vintage textiles and quilts gives them a second life. Quilting is a time-honored tradition that has been passed down through generations. Using these historic pieces in your clothing is a way to connect with that tradition while also preserving a piece of history in a practical way. By creating clothing from quilts and vintage fabrics, you're saving pieces of art that might otherwise have been discarded due to damage and carelessness or simply lost to time.

WHEN TO CUT

When working with vintage materials, it's important to honor the maker who originally created those materials. This means being mindful of how you cut and use the fabric. Knowing when to cut and when not to cut vintage materials can be tricky. On the one hand, you want to make the most of the material available to you, but on the other hand, it's important to preserve the integrity and history of the original quilt.

In general, it's a good idea to preserve any unique features or characteristics of the quilt or textile. A good rule of thumb, and a rule we stand by here at Kitty Badhands: If the quilt is in pristine condition and can still serve its original purpose as a quilt, leave it be! Always ask permission when cutting into a quilt whose origins you know—you don't want to upset the original maker or their family! If you do find a piece that you've decided to upcycle, be sure to cut into it in a way that minimizes waste and preserves as much of the original material as possible.

TOOLS AND MATERIALS

Tools

Sewing Machine: You need a basic sewing machine that can handle thicker fabrics, because upcycled quilts will have uneven batting, layered seams, and a variety of textures. We recommend the Juki TL-2000Qi, because it has been able to sew through thicker materials more easily than any other home sewing machines we've come across. It's a real workhorse, but it is on the pricier end of home sewing machines, so if you're newer to sewing, or just looking to test the waters in terms of sewing with quilts, the Singer Heavy Duty is a more budget-friendly option that still gets the job done.

Serger: Serged seams add a professional finish to any garment and keep fabrics (especially quilts, which have many layers) from fraying. We love the Juki MO-654DE, because it cuts and serges through thicker fabrics a bit more easily than its competitors. If you don't have a serger, you can finish seams with pinking shears, or use the zigzag stitch on your sewing machine to reinforce seams.

> **NOTE**
>
> If you plan to use a zigzag stitch, please note that the Juki TL-2000Qi is a straight-stitch-only machine and won't work for this method.

Sewing Machine and Serger Needles: You need both 80/12 and 110/18 sewing machine and serger needles. The 80/12 is a universal size that will work for most projects. The 110/18 needle can help with thicker fabrics or battings. Sometimes 110/18 serger needles can be hard to find. We use Schmetz universal needles for our serger.

Thread: For stitching thicker materials like quilts and wool blankets, you'll need a slightly thicker thread to keep things from snapping. Choose a 40-weight sewing machine thread (Signature, Aurifil, and Guterman make this weight of thread) for these projects. We find that the 40-weight thread also works well for all of our projects. For Serger thread, any standard serger/overlock thread will work, though Coats and Clark "Surelock" seems to be the sturdiest.

Pliers: ⅝″ (1.6cm) snap pliers are needed to attach snaps to the Jules Chore Coat (page 54) and the Elsie Cropped Coat (page 64). These snap pliers will also need a hole punch attachment. We love the Dritz ⅝″ (1.6cm) Snap Pliers because they come with the hole-punch attachment and all other necessary accessories (except the snaps!).

Cutting Tools: You need fabric scissors that can cut through thick materials. We use Fiskars 8″ forged stainless-steel blades. You may also choose to use a rotary cutter for some of the cutting steps. If you choose to use a rotary cutter, it will need to be at least 45mm to cut through thick materials, and you'll also need a cutting mat to protect your surfaces.

Basic Sewing Tools: As with most sewing projects, you'll also need an iron and ironing board, a ruler, a water soluble marker or pencil, and a cutting board.

Materials

Vintage Quilts and Wool Blankets: These thicker vintage textiles are perfect for the majority of the projects in this book. Take note of the required dimensions for each project so you choose the correct textile.

For more on using and sourcing these materials, see Finding Quilts and Vintage Textiles (page 16) and Working with Vintage Textiles (page 24).

Quilt Tops, Tablecloths, Bedsheets, Deadstock Fabric: Thinner vintage textiles are perfect for the Donna Dress (page 78) and the Drea Tank Top (page 86), because they provide breathability for warmer weather and the kind of flowy drape that you want in a summer wardrobe staple. Once again, you'll want to make sure you have enough material to work with for any given project, so look for the dimensions needed before starting to cut the pattern pieces.

For more on using and sourcing these materials, see Finding Quilts and Vintage Textiles (page 16) and Working with Vintage Textiles (page 24).

Closures: Zippers, snaps, and buttons add a nice finish to your projects. You'll need ⅝″ (1.6cm) metal snaps for the Jules Chore Coat (page 54) and Elsie Cropped Coat (page 64). Dritz is a great option for the snaps, especially if you're also using the Dritz Snap Pliers. You may also choose to opt for buttons instead of snaps for the coats. If so, we recommend at least ½″ (1.2cm)

buttons—anything smaller will have a hard time fitting through a buttonhole created on such thick material. You need a 9″ (22.9cm) zipper for the Jet Clutch (page 106).

Additional Fabrics: To line the Jet Clutch (page 106), you need a lightweight non-stretch fabric. We love Robert Kaufman Quilters Cotton because it is a high-quality cotton that comes in hundreds of colors. Shearling fabric, sometimes referred to as "sherpa," is needed for the Balaclava (page 114).

Twill Tape and Webbing/Belting: ¾″ (1.9cm) twill tape hides collar seams for both the Jules Chore Coat (page 54) and the Elsie Cropped Coat (page 64). We love Abbaoww Cotton Twill Tape Ribbon, which comes in a variety of colors. You also need 1″ (2.5cm) cotton webbing or belting to create the straps for the Avery Tote (page 100).

Bias Tape and Bias Tape Maker: You need single-fold ½″ (1.2cm) bias tape for the Drea Tank Top (page 86) and the Donna Dress (page 78). You need extra-wide double-fold ½″ (1.2cm) bias tape for the Holly Stocking (page 120), Jet Clutch (page 106), and as an option for if there are raw edges for the Jules Chore Coat (page 54), Elsie Cropped Coat (page 64), and Avery Tote (page 100).

We use Wrights Bias Tape, however you may decide that you would like to make your own. In that case, you'll need a 12mm bias tape maker to make the single-fold tape, and a 25mm bias tape maker to make the double-fold tape.

FINDING QUILTS AND VINTAGE TEXTILES

Finding the right materials for your upcycling project can be a challenge, but it's also part of the fun. Especially when it comes to upcycling quilts and vintage materials into clothing, finding the right materials is half the battle.

There are many factors to consider when choosing a textile; not every beautiful fabric you find may be a good candidate for creating upcycled clothing and accessories. But, after reading this chapter, you'll be well on your way to creating a unique and beautiful piece of clothing or accessory that you can be proud of.

Quilts

Quilts are a popular choice for upcycling because they often feature unique patterns and colors that can be incorporated into clothing or accessories. Quilts also offer the most beautiful incorporation of history within a project, because most quilts are handmade art pieces. However, it's essential to consider the thickness, design, and condition of the quilt before purchasing it for your project.

GOOD QUILT CANDIDATES

Thickness and Your Sewing Machine

Thicker materials may be more challenging to work with on a standard sewing machine. It's crucial to choose a material that your machine can handle. Before cutting out a whole project, we recommend taking a small piece of the potential material, layering it two or three times, and feeding it through your sewing machine. Whether this is possible will help you understand your machine's limits and choose the correct needle.

Damage vs. Size of the Project

Many vintage textiles come with varying degrees of damage and wear. With upcycling projects, a little bit of wear can add character and interest to your final piece. However, if the damage is extensive or if a majority of the material is damaged, it may be best to pass on that particular piece and keep searching for the perfect material for your project. Still, if you're working on a smaller project, you may be able to squeeze out enough material from a mostly damaged textile.

Quilt Pattern Scale vs. Size of the Project

When selecting a quilt or quilt top, consider the size of your project and the scale of the pieced pattern on the quilt. A large-scale pieced pattern may look beautiful as a whole, but if you're planning to create something smaller—such as a clutch or stocking—the beauty of the pattern may be lost when cutting out those smaller pieces. We recommend saving larger-scale patterns for larger projects—coats or dresses—that will have enough surface area to let the pieced quilt pattern shine. For more on matching the design of the piece with your project, see Pattern Placement (page 34).

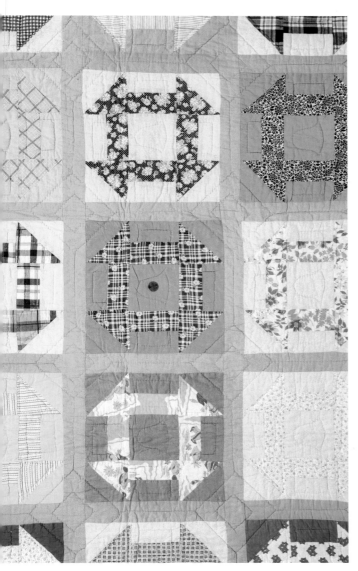

Larger-scale quilt pattern

Smaller-scale quilt pattern

QUILT TOPS

Quilt tops are the unfinished tops of quilts, made of pieced, patchwork fabric. They haven't been quilted to a batting or a backing fabric. They are often made from the same high-quality materials as finished quilts and can be an excellent option for upcycling into warmer-weather clothing items.

HAND-PIECED VS. MACHINE-PIECED QUILT TOPS

If you're working with a quilt top, make sure to check whether it was hand-pieced or machine-pieced. Hand-pieced quilt tops are sewn completely by hand, and each maker has a different way of stitching. Larger, loose hand stitches may not hold up well on an upcycled article of clothing, since clothing is pulled, stretched, and stressed as we wear it. Some makers create tight, secure hand stitches, but when in doubt, choose a quilt top that has been machine pieced.

Hand-stitched piecing

Wool Blankets

Wool blankets are another great option for upcycling because they are made from natural fibers and are durable enough to withstand wear and tear. However, just as with quilts, it's essential to consider the thickness of the blanket before making a purchase and starting a project.

Deadstock Fabrics

Deadstock fabrics are fabrics that were created for a company or designer but never sold or used in production. They are often vintage or limited edition and can be found online, or at independent and secondhand fabric stores. Because these fabrics were already produced and continue to sit unused, they're a sustainable option—using deadstock material, regardless of the fiber's contents, decreases the need for additional fabric production.

Shopping and Hunting for Vintage Materials

THRIFT STORES AND ANTIQUE SHOPS

Barge Canal Market

Thrift stores and antique shops can be a treasure trove of vintage materials, including quilts, wool blankets, and deadstock fabrics. Be sure to inspect each piece carefully before making a purchase—they are usually not returnable. Thrift stores, in particular, are great places to find quilts and other textiles with a low price tag.

ONLINE STORES/AUCTIONS

Online stores and auctions are another excellent option that can be accessed from the comfort of your own home. Websites like eBay and Etsy offer a wide selection of quilts and vintage materials. When bidding or purchasing, read the descriptions carefully and check out their return policies—not everything will arrive in the condition shown in the photographs. You can also send the seller a message to ask any particular questions you may have about the item's condition, size, or thickness before you buy it.

IN-PERSON AUCTIONS/ESTATE SALES

Keep an eye out for upcoming auctions or estate sales in your area! Attend them to see what treasures you might find. This is a particularly good option for those who enjoy "the hunt," as you never know what you may find. We recommend that you get there early!

YOUR OWN CLOSET

Don't overlook the potential of your closet (or a family member's closet). Not only is this a free option for finding vintage quilts and textiles, but it means that you'll be working with materials that have remarkable history and significance within your own family. Remember: ask for permission before cutting anything!

Get out there, explore your local thrift stores and estate sales, and let your creativity run wild!

WORKING WITH VINTAGE TEXTILES

Once you've chosen a quilt, blanket, quilt top, tablecloth, or other vintage textile to work with, it's time to prepare it for a project. This process is particularly important for quilts, and it starts by spending time with the quilt and getting to know it a little better. Spending time with the quilt before the cutting process not only allows you to make the necessary preparations, but also gives you the opportunity to feel close to the original maker of the quilt.

The first thing you'll want to pay attention to is the condition of the quilt: Does it have areas that need to be mended? Stains that need to be removed? What is the thickness and texture of the quilt?

You'll also get to spend some time examining the layout of the quilt: Does the pattern repeat? What's the pattern's scale? Perhaps there is an area of the quilt that really speaks to you and that you'll want to highlight in the finished project.

Working with Quilts

Quilts can often be trickier to work with than store-bought fabrics because each one is unique in its condition, thickness, and size. It's important to note a few characteristics about your quilt before getting started.

BATTING CONDITION

First, it's important to check the condition of the quilt's batting. Batting is the fluffy stuff that makes up the middle layer of the "quilt sandwich." If you're just working with a quilt top, it won't have batting. Vintage quilts have been used and loved and will not be in perfect condition. If your quilt has a little lumping and shifting in the batting, that's okay!

But if the batting is extremely uneven, creating a landscape of lumpy and bare spots, your project will be irregular and unsturdy. Quilts with this kind of batting may not be great candidates for an upcycled project. This is a tricky decision. There is no "rule" for how lumpy the batting can be—it's up to your discretion—but in general, you want to use a quilt that still has some semblance of even batting.

Batting in good condition

Batting in poor condition

THICKNESS

Quilts are created in a range of thicknesses, making different quilts better for different projects. The number-one thing you want to determine is whether your sewing machine can handle the quilt in question. The more powerful and heavy-duty your machine, the thicker the quilt can be. Since you'll be doubling or even tripling up quilt pieces in different projects, we recommend that you layer a few small test pieces of the quilt and give them a run through your machine.

NOTE

Coats and balaclavas will require three layers of quilt pieces through your machine at once. Totes, clutches, and stockings will require two layers of quilt pieces through your machine at once. Test your quilt accordingly before choosing which project you'll use it for.

It's also important to think about the kind of structure and movement you'd like your project to have. A quilt that is too thick will create a coat that doesn't have a lot of drape—it will come out quite stiff looking. However, a thicker quilt will add a nice structure to a clutch or tote bag. If you're using a non-heavy-duty sewing machine, thinner summer-weight quilts will be better candidates for you. The same is true if you're making a jacket for spring or summer.

SIZE CONSTRAINTS

Quilts come in all different sizes that make them suitable for different projects. Before making your first cut, lay out all of the pattern pieces on top of the quilt to make sure there is enough material to use. Perhaps you have just enough material, but not enough wiggle room to place the pattern pieces in a way that creates a balanced and/or symmetrical project, so we encourage you to experiment with the materials you have before cutting.

NOTE

Smaller quilt pieces, or the scraps left over from a larger project are great candidates for accessory projects. If one quilt is larger than you need for a project, try laying out the pattern pieces for two or even three projects on top of the quilt before you start to get the most out of the material.

Preparing a Quilt

REMOVING STAINS AND ODORS

Because you are working with a vintage material, chances are, it's going to need a little love before it's project ready. Many quilts come unwashed and may have yellowing, staining, and odors. While it may be impossible (and often not desirable) to get your quilt to look "brand new," it's important to get the quilt as clean as possible. This will also determine whether the quilt is actually sturdy enough to withstand washing in the first place—something that you'll definitely need to do with wearables.

OxiClean

OxiClean is a powerful tool for cleaning quilts and removing stains, but it also takes a toll on older fabrics. If you're going the OxiClean route, make sure that you're using a newer quilt, or one that's in fairly good condition. We recommend testing a small piece of the quilt in the OxiClean before soaking the entire quilt.

Place OxiClean in a bucket, plastic tub, or bathtub with hot water, and stir to dissolve; follow the instructions on the box for the right ratio of OxiClean to water. Submerge the quilt in the mixture and let it soak for up to 24 hours. After 24 hours, remove the quilt and either wash it on a gentle cycle with cold water or rinse it with cold water until the water runs clear.

> **NOTE**
>
> For stains that are small or concentrated in one area, you can use an OxiClean spray to treat the area before you soak it.

Vinegar Baths

Vinegar baths are a gentler approach to cleaning a quilt. They're a great way to remove any odors from the quilt but less effective at removing stains. They're also a great tool for stopping color bleeding. Just as with OxiClean, it's a good idea to test a bit of the textile in the vinegar bath before submerging the whole thing.

Add white distilled vinegar to a tub or container of cold water. Use approximately ½ cup of vinegar per gallon of water. Submerge the quilt for 15 to 30 minutes and then rinse it clean or put it through a gentle cycle with cold water in the washing machine.

NOTE

If a quilt has no signs of staining and does not have an odor, either hand wash it in cold water with a mild detergent or run it through a gentle cycle with cold water in the washing machine. After washing, either line dry or tumble dry it on low.

MENING

If a quilt has rips and tears, loose stitches, or worn-through fabric, you'll need to do a little mending. Complete mending *after* you've cut out the pattern pieces for a project; there's a good chance that you won't be using the entire quilt, and you may be able to just avoid damaged parts of the quilt instead of mending them. Mending after cutting the pattern pieces will ensure that you're not doing more work than you need to.

Hand Mending

Hand mending can be more time-consuming than machine mending, but it offers an opportunity for beautiful hand stitches that can add to the handmade quality of your piece. You can use this method and sewing thread to stitch together areas where the patchwork has come apart. Or, you can also choose a matching embroidery thread and create beautiful cross-stitches over the worn areas.

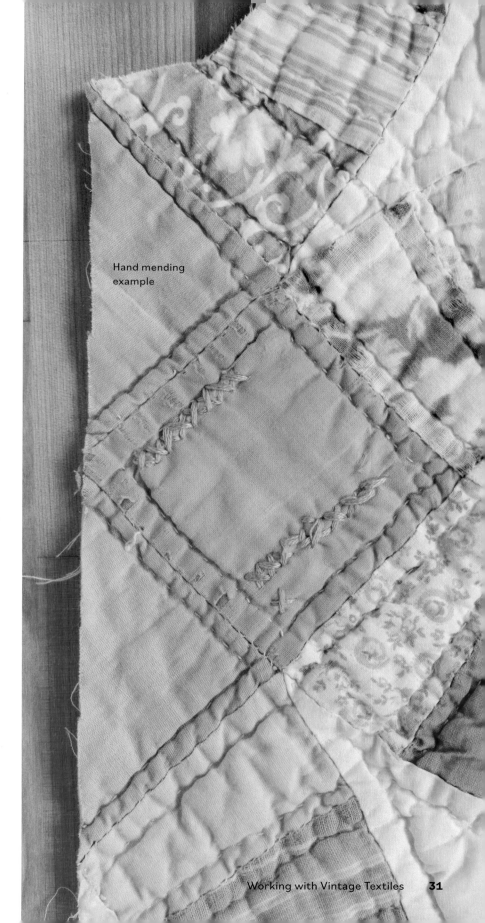

Hand mending example

Machine Mending

Machine mending won't give the quilt the look of a hand stitch, but it is much more time efficient, so if there is a lot of mending to do, it may be a better option for you. Use the zigzag stitch on your machine to bridge gaps, or run the zigzag stitch back and forth over worn-out fabrics that are falling apart.

Appliqué Mending

Sometimes a quilt block is missing completely, there is a hole in the quilt, or the fabric piece that needs mending is too fragile to withstand stitching. For these issues, appliqué is a wonderful option. With this technique, place a piece of new fabric over the old and sew it down—machine or hand stitching both work.

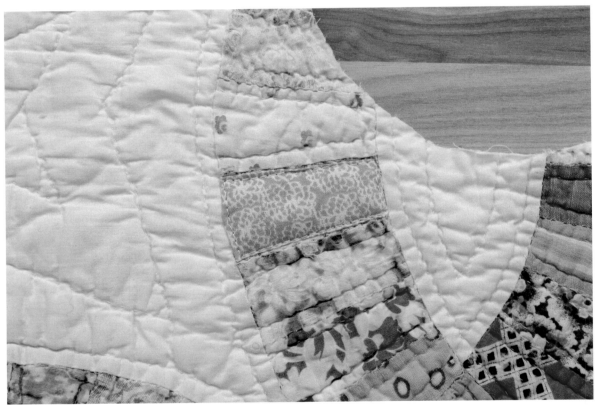

A piece of fabric has been appliquéd over a distressed area of the quilt, keeping in line with the original pattern.

To create a matching appliqué piece that blends into the original quilt, trace the shape of the area that needs appliqué. Place a piece of translucent paper or fabric on top of the quilt. Draw the shape and add ¼″ (6mm) around all sides. Transfer the shape to the appliqué fabric, and cut it out. Use an iron to fold the ¼″ (6mm) edge under so there are no raw edges. Place the prepared fabric piece on top of the area in need of mending and sew it down with your sewing machine or by hand. Feel free to pin if needed.

QUILT ROT

There is a difference between a quilt that has a few pieces of worn-out fabric and a quilt that is beyond repair. If a quilt feels fragile, has many small tears, and has worn fabric throughout, you might be dealing with quilt rot. Quilt rot refers to an invisible fungus that grows on a quilt when it's stored in a moist environment. It essentially makes the fabric so weak that it will continue to erode no matter how much mending you do.

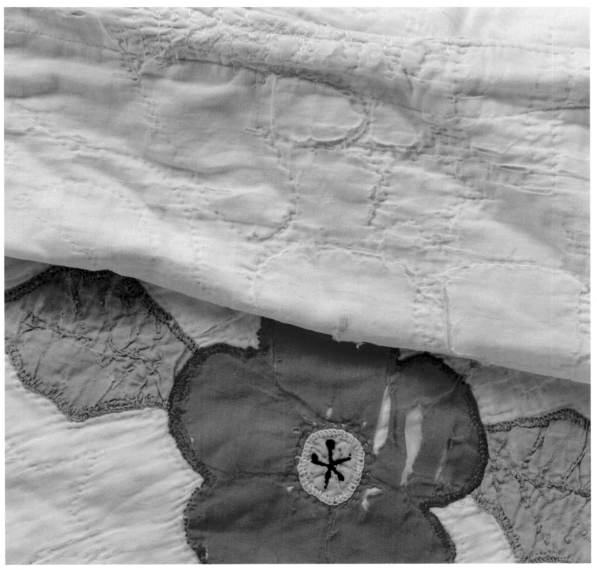

Quilt rot

Hold the top layer of the quilt and pull it in several directions. If the fabric easily rips apart, then you are, unfortunately, dealing with quilt rot. The quilt is not a good candidate for any project.

PATTERN PLACEMENT:
UTILIZING A QUILT'S LAYOUT TO CREATE BEAUTY

You've found your quilt, treated it for stains, and have made the necessary repairs; now it's time to lay out your project's pattern pieces to create a beautiful, one-of-a-kind work of wearable art. No two quilts are alike; each one will have distinct characteristics that should be admired and considered when deciding which parts to use for your project.

Take the time to note your quilt's pattern: Does it repeat? How are the different fabric patterns or colors placed throughout? Are there any particular areas of the quilt that are unique or that you are drawn to and want to highlight? Take the time to get to know the quilt or vintage material before cutting, and play around with laying out the pattern pieces over your quilt in various ways to visualize how each piece will fit together before making the first cut.

Scale

We talked a bit about scale already, but let's dive deeper. The scale of the individual shapes that make up the quilt is very important in determining the project for which the quilt will be used. Perhaps you were hoping to turn your quilt into a beautiful tote, but when you lay out the pattern pieces, you realize that the shapes are too large to be captured with a project that size. Generally, more miniature-scale quilts, like checkerboard patterns, are better for smaller projects, and larger-scale quilts, like wedding-ring patterns, work better for projects with more surface area. However, this isn't a hard-and-fast rule. If there is just a tiny piece of a larger quilt that you want to capture, then perhaps a larger-scale quilt works perfectly for a smaller project. Either way, it's essential to lay out your pattern pieces before cutting to understand what will be captured and lost once you cut.

Symmetry

Many quilts rely on sewing together *quilt blocks*, which results in a quilt that displays a repeated pattern. When a pattern is repeated, there is an opportunity to create symmetry, which can lend itself to making a project look balanced. For example, each coat project will need two front pieces. Laying these front pieces over matching parts of the original quilt design versus laying them randomly creates two different looks.

An example of matching coat fronts that create a symmetrical look

An example of coat fronts that have been laid out at random and are asymmetrical

As with all art, there are no rules, and perhaps the asymmetrical look is more appealing to you; the important thing to remember is to be intentional and visualize what the cut pattern piece will look like.

One Quilt, Infinite Layouts

Because each quilt is unique, there are endless possibilities for how the finished project might look, but also, because each quilt is unique, only one of these possibilities can be brought to life. It is essential to lay out all of the pattern pieces together before cutting them.

The most important reason for doing so is to ensure that the quilt is large enough to have room for each piece (sometimes this requires adjusting where and how closely together you're laying the pattern pieces), but also so that you can get an idea of how each project piece will come together to form a whole.

Layout A

Here, we have one quilt and two examples of layouts for the Jules Chore Coat (page 54). Both create balance and symmetry, utilizing the most exciting parts of the quilt pattern, yet, when assembled, each would look like an entirely different coat.

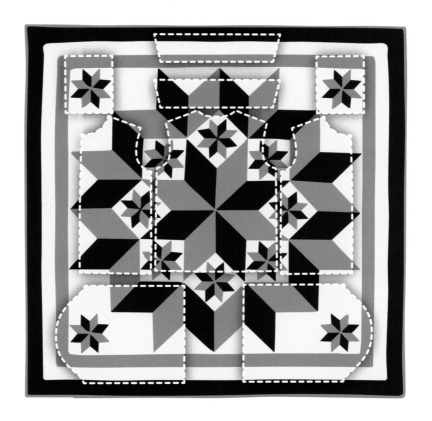

Layout B

In Layout A, the bottom edge of the front and back coat pieces line up with the edge of the quilt, and the front pieces also line up with the edge of the quilt on the sides. Because of this, the binding from the quilt will act as the binding for the edges of the coat, and no bias tape will need to be added to the project. The same is true for the sleeve ends on this layout. If attaching bias tape is intimidating or unappealing to you, aligning your pattern pieces to utilize the natural binding of the quilt might be the way to go for you, because in general it creates a more accessible first project.

The pockets in Layout A also match up perfectly with the pattern on the coat front, creating a seamless pattern, and the pocket is almost hidden, not appearing to be a separate element. This can be an excellent way to create a feeling of flow through the project. To achieve this effect, simply cut around the pocket markings on the coat's front pieces so that you can see the pattern beneath the coat's front pattern piece. This will allow you to find another part of the quilt that matches that section to lay the pocket piece over.

> **NOTE**
> It is very hard to get the pocket to line up 100 percent, so have patience and find a balance between putting the pocket where the pattern says it should go and where the pattern lines up the best.

LAYOUT B

Layout B places the pattern pieces more centrally on the quilt. On some quilts, like this one, a center point of the pattern is meant to be the focus. Laying the back pattern piece over the center of the quilt is a great way to capture that central and often very interesting piece of the quilt pattern. Laying the two front pieces directly next to the back piece keeps the pattern from being broken up along the side seams of the coat and creates a lovely flow around the coat. Because these pattern pieces are laid out in the center and not the edges of the quilt, this layout would need bias tape added to the edges as a step in the construction process (which is a part of the project instructions).

Sometimes it's impossible to find a way for the pocket to line up with the front coat pieces; other times it's just not the direction the coat wants to take artistically. A pocket that stands out instead of blending in can be a great way to add visual interest to the coat. In Layout B, we've chosen the eight-pointed star to be the central focus of the pocket so it can shine as its own element.

Remember, there is no right or wrong way to lay out the pattern pieces, but you only get one shot, so take your time, play around, and make it count!

SEWING TECHNIQUES

Each project in this book has step-by-step instructions, but some of the same sewing techniques will be used in multiple projects. When these techniques come into play, we'll ask you to refer to the corresponding techniques in this chapter to complete those steps.

Bias Tape

FINISH NECKLINES AND ARMHOLES WITH BIAS TAPE

A few of the projects in this book require you to finish necklines and armholes. This is done using single fold ½″ (1.2cm) bias tape. If you'd like to make your own bias tape, do so using a 12mm bias tape maker.

1   Unfold one crease of the prefolded bias tape on the right-hand side. Fold the short top edge of the bias tape over ½″ (1.2cm), wrong sides together. Press with the iron to keep it in place. *fig. A*

2   Turn the project inside out. With the right side of the bias tape and the right side of the project together, line up the edge of the bias tape with the edge of the armhole or neckline. Pin if needed. *fig. B*

3   Sew on top of the first lengthwise crease in the bias tape, ensuring that the edges of the tape and project stay lined up as you go. *fig. C*

4 When the end of the bias tape reaches where you started to sew, lay the end of the bias tape over the beginning of the bias tape and continue to sew until they overlap by ½″ (1.2cm). Trim off any excess tape. *fig. D*

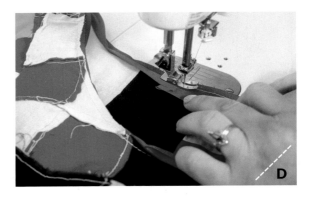

5 Turn the project right side out.

6 Fold the bias tape over the edge to the wrong side of the project.

7 Where the bias tape ends meet, unfold the underneath piece of bias tape, and then refold the crease over the raw-edged bias tape piece lying on top. This will create a seamless finish. *figs. E & F*

8 With the lengthwise crease of the outer edge of the bias tape still folded, topstitch the bias tape to the wrong side of the project, as close to the edge as possible. *fig. G*

ATTACHING BIAS TAPE TO AN EDGE

Most quilts already come with finished binding around the edges. When cutting out the pieces for a coat, if you place the front coat pieces at each corner of the quilt, the back coat pieces along the bottom edge, and the sleeve ends along the bottom edge, your pieces will already be finished with the binding from the original quilt itself. See Pattern Placement (page 34) for examples of this.

But if you cut any of those pattern pieces from the center portion of the quilt instead, you'll need to add your own binding. For this technique, we'll be using extra-wide double-fold ½″ (1.2cm) bias tape, or you can choose to make your own bias tape with a 25mm bias tape maker.

1   Unfold one crease of the bias tape and place it along the top edge of the textile, with the right side of the bias tape against the wrong side of the textile. *fig. A*

2   Line up the edge of the bias tape with the edge of the textile, and begin to sew in the first crease of the bias tape. Stop sewing ¼″ (6mm) before a corner. *fig. B*

Sleeves and Tote Bag Openings ▶ No corners here! Simply follow the steps in Attaching Bias Tape to an Edge (page 43) and Finish Bias Tape (page 45). Start at one side of the sleeve or tote pattern piece and bind across to the other side.

Bias Tape Corners

1 Turn the textile and sew diagonally from the stitch line to the corner point at a 45-degree angle. Backstitch when you reach the edge. *fig. A*

2 Fold the bias tape to be perpendicular along the 45-degree angled sewing line. *fig. B*

3 Fold the bias tape back down again, perpendicular in the other direction, lining up the fold of the bias tape with the edge of the front of the textile. *fig. C*

4 Starting at the folded edge, sew in the first crease in the bias tape just as before, continuing until you reach ¼˝ (6mm) before the next corner. Repeat Steps 1–4 for all corners. *fig. D*

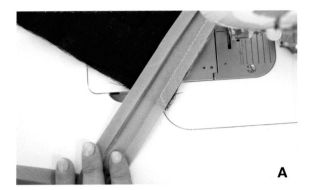

A

B

C

D

FINISH BIAS TAPE

1 Fold the bias tape over to the right side of the textile. *fig. A*

2 Make sure the edge of the bias tape just covers the stitch line.

3 Topstitch the edge of the bias tape to the front of the textile. Stop sewing 1″ (2.5cm) from the corner. *fig. B*

Finish Bias Tape Corners

1 Create a 45-degree angle at the end of the folded bias tape by folding it away from the textile. *fig. A*

2 Fold the bias tape in toward the textile along the perpendicular side of the corner so it meets up and forms a 45-degree angle. Pin as needed. *fig. B*

3 Resume topstitching along the original edge until you enter the ditch of the corner, formed by the folded bias tape.

4 With your needle in the ditch, turn the project 90 degrees and continue sewing along the next side of the bias tape edge. Stop sewing 1˝ (2.5cm) from the next corner, and repeat Steps 1–4. *fig. C*

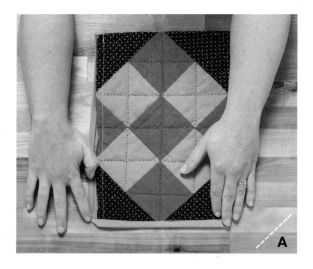

Attaching Snaps

MATERIALS

⅝″ (1.6cm) metal snaps

Heavy-duty snap pliers for ⅝″ (1.6cm) snaps

Water-soluble marker or pencil

Fabric pieces to attach

Pattern piece with snap placement

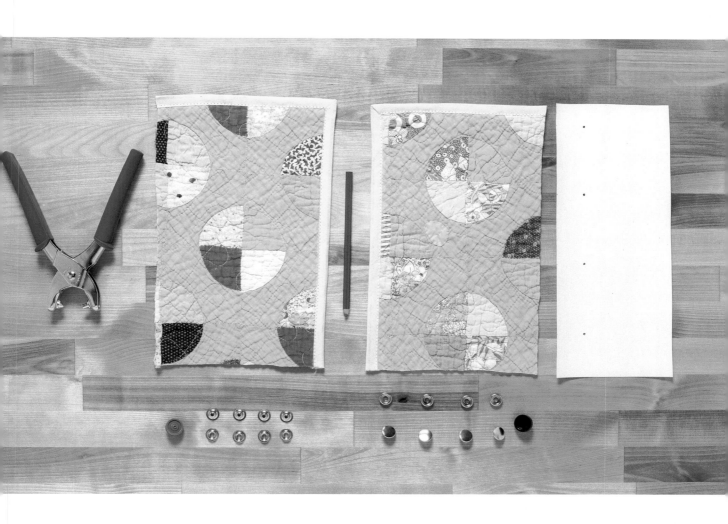

1 Using the water-soluble marker, mark the location of the snaps on the fabric pieces. The pattern indicates where they should be placed. *fig. A*

2 Use the snap pliers with the hole punch attachment to punch each of the marked spots. *fig. B*

3 Insert the snap top caps through each hole, on the right side of the project. Place the top sockets on the other side of the project, aligning them with the top caps. Use the snap pliers to secure the top cap to the top socket. *figs. C–D*

4 Insert the snap bottom posts through each hole on the other piece, on the wrong side of the project. Place the bottom studs on the other side of the project, aligning them with the bottom posts. Use snap pliers to secure the bottom posts to the bottom studs. *figs. E–G*

NOTE

We love snaps! But there are other great options for closures, too. If your machine has a buttonhole feature and can withstand the weight of the material, buttons are another option that will add visual interest to your piece. Many craft stores also sell various toggles that can be sewn onto your project as a closure option.

E

F

G

Finishing Seams

Many of the projects in this book call for the use of an overlock machine or serger. While we love the look of a professionally finished seam, we understand that not everyone will have access to one of these machines. Whenever a project calls for serged seams, a good alternative method for finishing seams is to use the zigzag stitch on a sewing machine. We recommend playing around a little with the width of the stitch until you find a setting that places one edge of the zigzag just over the edge of the project and the other edge near the seam, making it about the width of the seam allowance.

Cutting Quilt Coat Backs ▶ For both the Jules Chore Coat (page 54) and the Elsie Cropped Coat (page 64), the back pattern piece instructs you to cut it on the fold. Feel free to skip this section, and cut the pieces out as directed. We prefer to cut out this piece on one layer. To do this, lay out the back pattern piece on the textile as desired, face up. Use a marking tool to outline the pattern piece. Then flip the pattern piece over along the center back line, mirroring it. Outline the pattern piece again, creating the full back. The two halves should share the center back line. Then cut out the back following the outline on one layer. Do not cut on the center back line.

PROJECTS

To access the pattern PDFs for all of the projects in this section, scan the QR codes or go to the tiny urls below:

Full-Size patterns for printing at a copy shop:
tinyurl.com/11542-pattern1-download

Letter-Size patterns for printing at home:
tinyurl.com/11542-pattern2-download

Of the garment projects, only the Jules Chore Coat is designed for a unisex fit. The other garment projects are women's cut, and we suggest using the women's size chart.

UNISEX SIZE CHART

Size (name)	Size (number)	Chest Measurement	Waist Measurement	Hip Measurement
X-Small	0–2	30″–32″ (76.2–81.3cm)	24″–26″ (61–66cm)	30″–32″ (76.2–81.3cm)
Small	4–6	34″–36″ (86.4–91.4cm)	28″–30″ (71.1–76.2cm)	34″–36″ (86.4–91.4cm)
Medium	8–10	38″–40″ (96.5–101.6cm)	32″–34″ (81.3–86.4cm)	38″–40″ (96.5–101.6cm)
Large	12–14	42″–44″ (106.7–111.8cm)	36″–38″ (91.4–96.5cm)	42″–44″ (106.7–111.8cm)
X-Large	16–18	46″–48″ (116.8–121.9cm)	40″–42″ (101.6cm–106.7cm)	46″–48″ (116.8–121.9cm)
XX-Large	20–22	50″–52″ (127–132.1cm)	43″–45″ (109.2cm–114.3cm)	50″–52″ (127–132.1cm)

WOMEN'S SIZE CHART

Size (name)	Size (number)	Bust Measurement	Waist Measurement	Hip Measurement
X-Small	0–2	30″–32″ (76.2–81.3cm)	23″–25″ (58.4–63.5cm)	32″–34″ (81.3–86.4cm)
Small	4–6	33″–35″ (83.8–88.9cm)	26″–28″ (66–71.1cm)	35″–37″ (88.9–94cm)
Medium	8–10	36″–38″ (91.4–96.5cm)	29″–31″ (73.7–78.7cm)	38″–40″ (96.5–101.6cm)
Large	12–14	39″–41″ (99.1–104.1cm)	32″–34″ (81.3–86.4cm)	41″–43″ (104.1cm–109.2cm)
X-Large	16–18	42″–44″ (106.7–111.8cm)	35″–37″ (88.9–94cm)	44″–46″ (111.8–116.8cm)
XX-Large	20–22	45″–47″ (114.3–119.4cm)	38″–40″ (96.5–101.6cm)	47″–49″ (119.4–124.5cm)

MEASURING

Chest/Bust: Using a flexible tape measure, measure under your arms, around the fullest part of your chest.

Waist: Using a flexible tape measure, measure around your natural waistline, below your rib cage, leaving the tape slightly loose.

Hip: Using a flexible tape measure, measure around the fullest part of your body, above the tops of your legs.

Jules Chore Coat

THE JULES CHORE COAT IS A KITTY BADHANDS SIGNATURE AND WAS THE FIRST PIECE EVER CREATED FOR OUR LINE. IT'S A UNISEX-FIT COAT DESIGNED TO LOOK GREAT ON EVERY BODY TYPE. FEATURING A BOXY, OVERSIZE FIT, DEEP FRONT POCKETS, AND SLIGHTLY WIDER ARMS, THIS COAT IS THE PERFECT PATTERN TO SHOW OFF JUST ABOUT ANY QUILT AND CAN BE MADE WITH THINNER QUILTS FOR COOL SUMMER NIGHTS OR THICK QUILTS AND WOOL BLANKETS TO KEEP YOU COZY ALL WINTER LONG. TO SHARE YOUR PROJECT, USE **#julesquiltedchorecoat**

MATERIALS

Note that bias tape is an optional material for this project. See Bias Tape (page 41) to determine if you need bias tape.

Vintage quilt (at least 65″ × 70″/165.1 × 177.8cm)

30″ (76.4cm) piece of ¾″ (1.9cm) twill tape

6 sets of ¾″ (1.9cm) metal snaps

40-weight cotton sewing machine thread

4 cones serger thread

1 package extra-wide double-fold ½″ (1.2cm) bias tape (optional)

TOOLS

Water soluble marker or pencil

Scissors

Sewing machine

Serger

110/18 sewing machine needle

110/18 serger needles

Iron

Snap pliers

CUTTING LIST

Cut 1 Jules Chores Coat Back (on fold).

Cut 2 Jules Chore Coat Front (mirrored).

Cut 2 Jules Chore Coat Sleeve.

Cut 2 Jules Chore Coat Pocket.

Cut 2 Jules Chore Coat Collar.

Optional: Cut 1 Elsie Cropped Coat Snap Marker

Construction

Unless otherwise noted, use a ⅜″ (1cm) seam allowance for all seams. For alternatives to finishing seams without a serger, see Finishing Seams (page 51). Transfer all pattern marks onto the cut fabric pieces.

POCKETS

1 Serge around the entire perimeter of each pocket. *fig. A*

2 Fold the top of one pocket under to the wrong side by 1″ (2.5cm). Press and pin. *fig. B*

3 With the pocket facing wrong side up, sew the fold in place on the edge, directly over the serged seam. *fig. C*

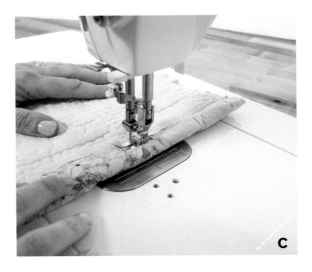

4 Place the pocket on the ironing board, wrong side up. Fold the bottom edge up to the wrong side about ¼″ (6mm) so the serged seam doesn't show on the front. Press. Then repeat with the sides of the pocket. Repeat Steps 2–4 for the second pocket. *fig. D*

5 Using the pattern markings as a guide, place one pocket on one front, and pin it in place. The wrong side of the pocket should face the right side of the front piece. *fig. E*

6 Starting at the top of the pocket and as close to the edge as possible, topstitch the pocket down to the front piece around three edges (side, bottom, side), making sure to backstitch several times at the beginning and end for pocket sturdiness. At each corner, stop with the needle in the fabric and rotate the pieces to continue across the next side. *fig. F*

7 Repeat Steps 5–6 for the second pocket and second front.

D

E

F

ASSEMBLE THE CHORE COAT

1   With the right sides together, line up the front piece shoulders with the shoulders of the back piece. Pin in place.

2   Sew the fronts and back together at the shoulder seams. Serge the seam allowances. *fig. A*

3   If the sleeve ends are raw and need bias tape on the bottom edge, attach it now by following the instructions in Attaching Bias Tape to an Edge (page 43).

4   With the right sides together, pin the centers of the sleeve to the center shoulder seams. Then continue to pin the tops of the sleeves in place along the armhole opening. *fig. B*

5   Sew the sleeves to the body of the coat. Serge the seam allowance. *fig. C*

6   With right sides together, pin along the side seam and sleeve seam. Start at the end of the sleeve and pin the back of the coat to the front of the coat along the edge until you reach the bottom of the coat.

7   Repeat Step 6 on the other side of the coat.

8   Sew both sides of the coat together. Serge the seam allowance. *fig. D*

9   If the bottom and front edges of the coat need bias tape, attach it now by following the instructions in Attaching Bias Tape to an Edge (page 43).

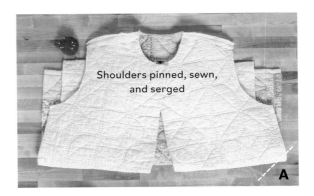

Shoulders pinned, sewn, and serged

A

B

C

D

PREPARE AND ATTACH THE COLLAR

1 Place the collar pieces on top of one another, right sides together. Pin in place.

2 Sew the short sides and top (wider edge) of the collar pieces together, leaving the bottom open.

3 Trim off the corners of the collar, making sure not to cut through the stitches. *fig. A*

Collar sewn at sides and
top, and corners trimmed

A

4 Flip the collar right side out and press.

5 Topstitch around the sides and top of the collar, ¼˝ (6mm) from the edge. The bottom should remain open. *fig. B*

6 Lay the twill tape lengthwise along the bottom of the collar, matching the edge of the tape with the edge of the collar. Make sure there are several extra inches of twill tape on each end (the twill tape measurement is long enough to accommodate up to a XXL coat, so depending on the size of the coat being constructed, you'll have more or less extra). Pin in place. *fig. C*

B

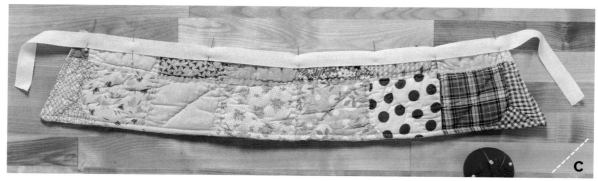

C

7 Using a ¼″ (6mm) seam allowance, sew the twill tape to the bottom length of the collar. *fig. D*

8 With the twill tape side facing up, match the center of the collar with the right side of the center of the back of the coat and pin the whole length of the collar to the neckline. *fig. E*

9 Trim the twill tape so there is only an extra 1″ (2.5cm) extending beyond the coat at each end.

10 Fold the 1″ (2.5cm) of twill tape at each end over toward the center of the coat and on top of the existing strip of twill tape so the new folded edge lines up with the front edges of the coat.

11 Sew the collar to the neckline of the coat, as close to the edge as possible, starting at the front edge of the coat and stitching the folded twill tape down, and continuing to the other front edge. *fig. F*

12 Fold the twill tape down toward the inside of the coat, over the neckline seam so it hides the raw edge of the neckline. Pin in place. If at any point the neckline edge is frayed or sticks out past the twill tape, you may need to trim it. *fig. G*

13 Sew the twill tape down over the neckline seam to the body of the coat, as close to the edge of the twill as possible. *fig. H*

14 Using the pattern markings as a guide, attach snaps to the front pieces by following the instructions in Attaching Snaps (page 47).

Elsie Cropped Coat

THE ELSIE CROPPED COAT IS A WOMEN'S CUT COAT. IT HAS A CROPPED AND FITTED SILHOUETTE, AND BECAUSE OF THIS, IT CAN BE MADE USING QUILTS THAT ARE MUCH SMALLER THAN THE JULES CHORE COAT (PAGE 54). THIS PATTERN WORKS WELL FOR MOST QUILT DESIGNS, BUT ESPECIALLY FOR SMALLER TO MEDIUM-SIZE MOTIFS. IT MAKES A REALLY GREAT SPRING QUILTED COAT OR FALL WOOL COAT. BECAUSE IT'S A MORE STRUCTURED COAT, WE USUALLY RECOMMEND SHYING AWAY FROM EXTREMELY THICK QUILTS OR BLANKETS; OTHERWISE, THE PATTERN CAN COME OUT LOOKING A LITTLE STIFF AND MISSING THE SATISFYING COMFORT AND DRAPE THAT COMES WITH USING A THINNER QUILT. TO SHARE YOUR PROJECT, USE **#elsiequiltedcoat**

MATERIALS

Note that bias tape is an optional material for this project. See Bias Tape (page 41) to determine if you need bias tape.

Vintage quilt (at least 55″ × 65″/139.7 × 165.1cm)

30″ (76.2cm) piece of ¾″ (1.9cm) twill tape

6 sets of ¾″ (1.9cm) metal snaps

40-weight cotton sewing machine thread

4 cones serger thread

1 package extra-wide double-fold ½″ (1.2cm) bias tape (optional)

TOOLS

Water soluble marker or pencil

Scissors

Sewing machine

Serger

110/18 sewing machine needle

110/18 serger needles

Iron

Snap pliers

CUTTING LIST

Cut 1 Elsie Cropped Coat Back (on fold).

Cut 2 Elsie Cropped Coat Front (mirrored).

Cut 2 Elsie Cropped Coat Sleeve.

Cut 2 Elsie Cropped Coat Pocket.

Cut 2 Elsie Cropped Coat Collar.

Optional: Cut 1 Elsie Cropped Coat Snap Marker

Construction

Unless otherwise noted, use a ⅜˝ (1cm) seam allowance for all seams. For alternatives to finishing seams without a serger, see Finishing Seams (page 51). Transfer all pattern marks onto the cut fabric pieces.

POCKETS

1 Serge around the entire perimeter of each pocket. *fig. A*

2 Fold the long diagonal edge of the pocket under to the wrong side by ½˝ (1.2cm), press, and pin.

3 With the wrong side of the pocket facing down, sew the fold in place on the edge, directly over the serged seam. *fig. B*

4 Place the pocket on the ironing board, wrong side up. Fold up the two sides to the wrong side about ¼˝ (6mm) so the serged seam doesn't show on the front. Press. Then repeat with the top and bottom sides. Repeat Steps 2–4 for the second pocket. *fig. C*

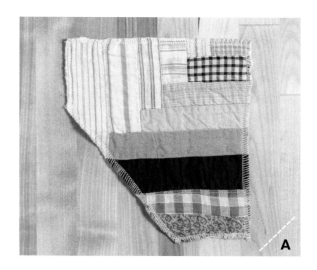

A

B

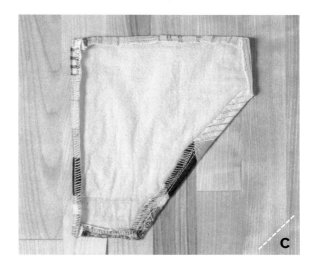

C

5 Using the pattern markings as a guide, place one pocket on one front, and pin it in place. The wrong side of the pocket should face the right side of the front piece. *fig. D*

6 Starting at the top of the pocket and as close to the edge as possible, topstitch the pocket down to the front piece on all edges except the diagonal one, making sure to backstitch several times at the beginning and end for pocket sturdiness. At each corner, stop with the needle in the fabric and rotate the pieces to continue across the next side. *fig. E*

7 Repeat Steps 5–6 for the second pocket and second front.

ASSEMBLE THE CROPPED COAT

1 With the right sides together, line up the front piece shoulders with the shoulders of the back piece. Pin in place.

2 Sew the fronts and back together at the shoulders. Serge the seam allowances. *fig. A*

3 If the sleeves have raw ends and need bias tape on the bottom edges, attach it now by following the instructions in Attaching Bias Tape to an Edge (page 43).

4 With the right sides together, pin the center of the sleeves to the center shoulder seams. Then continue to pin the top of the sleeves in place along the armhole openings. *fig. B*

5 Sew the sleeves to the body of the coat. Serge the seam allowance. *fig. C*

6 With right sides together, pin along the side seam and sleeve seam. Start at the end of the sleeve and pin the back of the coat to the front of the coat along the edge until you reach the bottom of the coat.

7 Repeat Step 6 on the other side of the coat.

8 Sew both sides of the coat together. Serge the seam allowance. *fig. D*

9 If the bottom and front edges of the coat need bias tape, attach it now by following the instructions in Attaching Bias Tape to an Edge (page 43).

PREPARE AND ATTACH THE COLLAR

1 Place the collar pieces on top of one another, right sides together. Pin in place.

2 Sew the short sides and top (wider edge) of the collar pieces together, leaving the bottom open. *fig. A*

3 Trim off the corners of the collar, making sure not to cut through the stitches. *fig. B*

4 Flip the collar right side out and press.

5 Topstitch around the sides and top of the collar, ¼″ (6mm) from the edge. The bottom should remain open. *fig. C*

6 Lay the twill tape lengthwise along the bottom of the collar, matching the edge of the tape with the edge of the collar and making sure there are several extra inches of twill tape on each end. Pin in place. *fig. D*

7 Using a ¼″ (6mm) seam allowance, sew the twill tape to the bottom length of the collar. *fig. E*

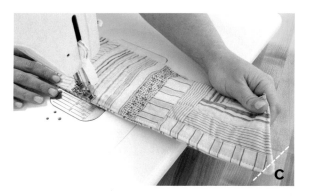

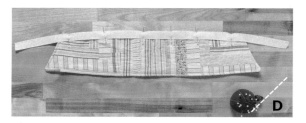

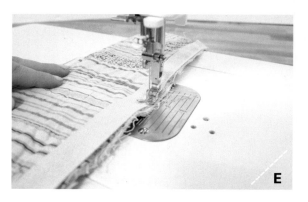

8 With the twill tape side facing up, match the center of the collar with the right side of the center of the back of the coat. Pin the collar in place from front edge to front edge. *fig. F*

9 Trim the twill tape so there is only an extra 1″ (2.5cm) extending beyond the coat at each end.

10 Fold the 1″ (2.5cm) of twill tape at each end over toward the center of the coat and on top of the existing strip of twill tape so the new folded edge lines up with the front edges of the coat.

11 Sew the collar to the neckline of the coat, starting at the front edge of the coat and stitching the folded twill tape down, and continuing to the other front edge. *fig. G*

12 Fold the twill tape down toward the inside of the coat, over the neckline seam so it hides the raw edge of the neckline. Pin in place. If at any point the neckline edge is frayed or sticks out past the twill tape, you may need to trim it. *fig. H*

13 Sew the twill tape down over the neckline seam to the body of the coat, as close to the edge of the twill as possible. *fig. I*

14 Using the pattern markings as a guide, attach the snaps to the front pieces by following the instructions in Attaching Snaps (page 47).

F

G

H

I

Mia Vest

SEASONLESS, VERSATILE, AND THE PERFECT WAY TO ADD EXTRA VISUAL INTEREST TO ANY OUTFIT, THE MIA VEST IS ONE OF OUR FAVORITE PATTERNS TO WARM UP WITH BEFORE HEADING INTO MORE COMPLICATED COAT SEWING PATTERNS. ITS CROPPED AND SLEEVELESS DESIGN MAKES IT AN EXCELLENT WAY TO UTILIZE A SMALLER BABY QUILT OR LARGER SCRAPS WHILE STILL BEING ABLE TO CREATE SOMETHING WEARABLE. TO SHARE YOUR PROJECT, USE **#miaquiltedvest**

MATERIALS

Vintage quilt or quilt scraps (at least 30″ × 60″/76.2 × 152.4cm)

40-weight cotton sewing machine thread

4 cones serger thread

1 package extra-wide double-fold ½″ (1.2cm) bias tape

TOOLS

Scissors

Sewing machine

Serger

110/18 sewing machine needle

110/18 serger needles

CUTTING LIST

Cut 1 Mia Vest Back (on fold).

Cut 2 Mia Vest Front (mirrored).

Construction

Unless otherwise noted, use a ⅜″ (1cm) seam allowance for all seams. For alternatives to finishing seams without a serger, see Finishing Seams (page 51).

1   With right sides together, pin the two fronts to the back at the shoulders and sides.

2   Sew the fronts and backs together at the shoulders and sides. Serge the seam allowances. *fig. A*

3   Unfold the bias tape. Fold over the tape by ½″ (1.2cm) on one short end, wrong sides together.

4   Place the folded end of the bias tape at the center of the back of the neck on the wrong side of the vest.

5   Starting at the neck, attach the bias tape to the whole vest (excluding the armholes), following the instructions in Attaching Bias Tape to an Edge (page 43). Skip the section about attaching bias tape to corners, because the vest has rounded edges. As you attach the bias tape, guide it around the curves. *fig. B*

6   To end the bias tape, overlap the strip by ½″ (1.2cm) with the folded starting point. Trim the excess. *figs. C & D*

A

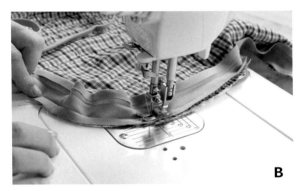

B

C

D

7 Where the bias tape overlaps on the back neck, unfold the unsewn long edge of the bottom piece. Then refold the crease, encompassing the top piece of bias tape. This will create a seamless finish when you fold the bias tape over to the right side of the vest. *figs. E–G*

8 Finish the bias tape by following the instructions in Finish Bias Tape (page 45).

9 To bind the armholes, start at the seam in the armpit and repeat steps 5–7 on both sides.

Pocket Hack ▶ Want a little extra storage in your Mia Vest? Try adding the pockets from the Elsie Cropped Coat (page 64) to the front pieces of the vest. Follow the instructions in Pockets (page 67) before starting Step 1 of the Mia Vest.

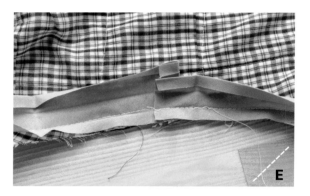

E

F

G

Donna Dress

IT'S TIME TO LET THE QUILT TOP YOU'VE FOUND REALLY SHINE IN THIS FLOWING DRESS PROJECT. IT'S ALSO A GREAT OPTION FOR THRIFTED SHEETS. DESIGNED TO BE FREE IN THE WAIST AND HIP, THIS DRESS LOOKS GREAT ON ALL BODY TYPES AND IS AS COMFORTABLE AS IT IS STYLISH. THE DONNA DRESS CAN BE MADE IN A LONG OR MINI VERSION, ALLOWING YOU TO CREATE TWO VERY DIFFERENT LOOKS WITH THE SAME PATTERN. WE LOVE PAIRING THIS DRESS WITH EITHER OF OUR COAT STYLES. TO SHARE YOUR PROJECT, USE **#donnaquilttopdress**

MATERIALS

Quilt top, tablecloth, or other vintage textile (at least 65″ × 65″/165.1 × 165.1cm)

37″ (94cm) single-fold ½″ (1.2cm) bias tape

40-weight cotton sewing machine thread in 2 colors

4 cones serging thread

> **NOTE**
> One color thread color will be used for the top thread and the other for the bottom bobbin when making gathering stitches to create the gathered skirt.

TOOLS

Water soluble marker or pencil

Scissors

Sewing machine

Serger

75/11 sewing machine needle

75/11 serger needle

Iron

CUTTING LIST

Cut 1 Donna Dress Bodice Front (on fold).

Cut 1 Donna Dress Bodice Back (on fold).

Cut 2 Donna Dress Sleeve (mirrored).

Cut 2 Donna Dress Skirt (on fold).

Construction

Unless otherwise noted, use a ⅜″ (1cm) seam allowance for all seams. As a reminder, for alternatives to finishing seams without a serger, see Finishing Seams (page 51). Transfer all pattern marks onto the cut fabric pieces.

CREATE THE BODICE WITH SLEEVES

1   With the right sides together, line up the front and back bodices at the shoulders. Pin in place.

2   Sew the front and back together at the shoulders. Serge the seam allowances. *fig. A*

3   Starting at a shoulder seam, attach bias tape to the neckline by following the instructions in Finish Necklines and Armholes with Bias Tape (page 41).

4   With the right sides together, match up the center mark of the sleeve to the shoulder seam and pin it in place around the arm opening. *fig. B*

5   Sew the sleeve to the bodice. Serge the seam allowance. *fig. C*

6   Repeat Steps 4–5 for the other sleeve.

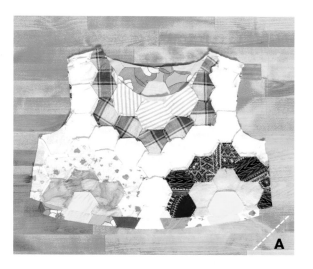

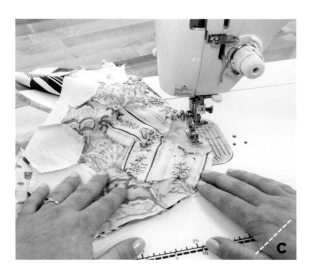

GATHERED SKIRT

1 Turn the tension on your sewing machine all the way down to zero and increase the stitch length to about 4. This will create a "gathering" stitch. Put the second thread color in the bottom bobbin.

2 Using a ¾″ (1.9cm) seam allowance, grab one skirt piece and stitch across the entire top of the piece. If done correctly, the top thread loop (see navy thread) should be exposed on the back of the skirt. Leave long tails on both ends. Repeat on the second skirt piece. *fig. A*

3 With the right sides together, pin the center top of one skirt piece to the center of the bottom front bodice. *fig. B*

4 Starting at one side of the skirt piece, pull the bottom thread of the gathering stitch so the skirt begins to cinch together. Push the cinching toward the center until the side of the skirt piece aligns with the side of the front bodice. *fig. C*

5 Repeat Step 4 on the other side.

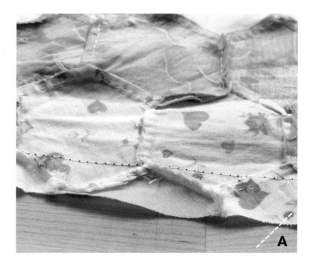

Skirt gathered to match up with bodice on one side

6 Adjust the gathering so the gathers are evenly distributed all the way across the skirt piece. Then pin the skirt in place along the bottom of the front bodice. *fig. D*

7 Repeat Steps 3–6 with the second skirt piece and back bodice.

8 Set your stitch length and tension back to their normal settings. Sew the attached skirt piece to the bottom of the front bodice. Serge the seam allowance.

9 Sew the attached skirt piece to the bottom of the back bodice. Serge the seam allowance. *fig. E*

10 Pull the bottom thread of the gathering stitches completely out, removing all the gathering stitches.

A

FINISH THE DRESS

1 Align the front of the dress and the back of the dress, right sides together.

2 Match the sides of the dress together so the bottom, waistline, and sleeve ends match up. Pin in place down from the sleeve ends to the bottom edge on both sides. *fig. A*

3 Sew from the sleeve ends to the bottom skirt edge on both sides of the dress. Serge both seam allowances. *fig. B*

4 Serge around the bottom hem of the skirt. *fig. C*

5 Fold the bottom hem under to the wrong side of the dress, so the serged seam is just turned under. Then turn under once more (twice total). Pin it in place. *fig. D*

B

C

D

6 Topstitch around the folded bottom hem of the skirt on the wrong side, as close to the bottom edge as possible. *fig. E*

7 Repeat Steps 4–6 to hem each sleeve.

Sleeve Hack ▸ Want longer sleeves for the dress? Simply lengthen the lines on each side of the sleeve pattern pieces to the length you'd like. This will create a beautiful wide, long sleeve!

E

Drea Tank

THE DREA TANK PATTERN WAS DESIGNED TO BE SIMPLE YET CLASSIC: A BLANK SLATE TO SHOW OFF THE BEAUTIFUL PATTERNS FEATURED ON YOUR COLLECTED TEXTILES. WITH CHEST DARTS FOR THE PERFECT FIT AROUND THE BUST, THIS TANK TOP ALSO FEATURES A STRAIGHT BOTTOM HEM, WHICH MAKES IT INCREDIBLY EASY TO LENGTHEN OR SHORTEN INTO A CROP TOP. THIS IS A GREAT PROJECT TO INCORPORATE THE USE OF VINTAGE TABLECLOTHS, WHICH ARE OFTEN TOO SMALL TO BE TURNED INTO A DRESS, OR TO USE YOUR QUILT TOP SCRAPS FROM THE DONNA DRESS PROJECT. TO SHARE YOUR PROJECT, USE **#dreaquilttoptank**

MATERIALS

Quilt top tablecloth, or other vintage textile (at least 48″ × 50″/121.9 × 127cm)

One 3-yard (2.8m) package single-fold ½″ (1.2cm) bias tape

40-weight cotton sewing machine thread

4 cones serger thread

TOOLS

Water soluble marker or pencil

Scissors

Sewing machine

Serger

75/11 sewing machine needle

75/11 serger needle

Iron

CUTTING LIST

Cut 1 piece bias tape 36″ (91.4cm).

Cut 2 pieces bias tape 27″ (68.6cm).

Cut 1 Drea Tank Front (on fold).

Cut 1 Drea Tank Back (on fold).

Construction

Unless otherwise noted, use a ⅜″ (1cm) seam allowance for all seams. As a reminder, for alternatives to finishing seams without a serger, see Finishing Seams (page 51). Transfer all pattern marks onto the cut fabric pieces.

ASSEMBLE THE TANK TOP

1 First, sew the darts. Wrong side up, hold the tank top bodice front at the point of one marked dart. Then fold (right sides together) the dart so that the dart marks on the edge of the bodice meet up. Pin. *fig. A*

2 Starting from the bodice edge, sew along the folded dart line to the point. Backstitch to hold in place. *fig. B*

3 With the right sides together, line up the front and back bodices at the shoulders. Pin in place.

4 Line up the front and back bodice sides. Pin. *fig. C*

5 Sew the shoulders together.

6 Sew the sides together.

7 Serge the shoulder and the side seams.

ATTACH BIAS TAPE

1 Starting at a shoulder seam, attach the 36″ (91.4cm) strip of bias tape to the neckline by following the instructions in Finish Necklines and Armholes with Bias Tape (page 41).

2 Starting at one side seam, attach a 27″ (68.6cm) strip of bias tape strips to each armhole by following the instructions in Finish Necklines and Armholes with Bias Tape (page 41).

FINISH THE TANK TOP

1 Serge around the bottom hem of the tank top. *fig. A*

2 Fold the bottom hem under twice, using the serged seam width as your guide for how large each fold should be. Pin. *fig. B*

3 Topstitch around the bottom hem, removing the pins as you sew as close to the folded edge as possible. *fig. C*

Tank Hack ▶ Turn the Drea Tank into a dress! Simply add the skirt pattern pieces from the Donna Dress (page 78) to the bottom hem of the Drea Tank. You may want to shorten the Drea tank to match the bodice length of the Donna Dress before attaching the skirt.

A

B

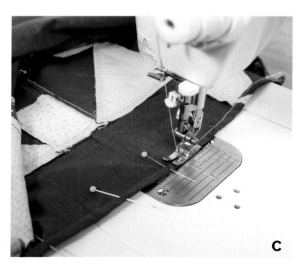

C

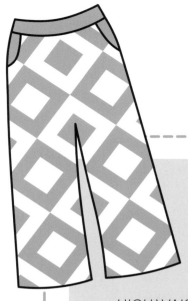

June Pants

HIGH WAISTED, WIDE LEG, AND A LITTLE ROOMY, THE JUNE PANTS ARE THE PERFECT PROJECT FOR SHOWING OFF LARGER SWATHS OF VINTAGE MATERIAL. THEY FEATURE AN ELASTIC WAISTBAND FOR AN ALL-DAY COMFORTABLE FIT AND FRONT SIDE POCKETS TO STASH YOUR HANDS OR YOUR WALLET. WE LOVE USING THE SAME TEXTILE FOR THE JUNE PANTS AND THE DREA TANK TO CREATE THE ULTIMATE MATCHING SET. TO SHARE YOUR PROJECT, USE **#junequiltedpants**

MATERIALS

Quilt top, tablecloth, or other vintage textile (at least 65″ × 65″/165.1 × 165.1cm)

40-weight cotton sewing machine thread

4 cones serging thread

2″ (5cm) wide elastic (length depends on size of pants; see below)

TOOLS

Water soluble marker or pencil

Scissors

Sewing machine

Serger

75/11 sewing machine needle

75/11 serger needle

Iron

CUTTING LIST

Cut 2 June Pants Front (mirrored).

Cut 2 June Pants Back (mirrored).

Cut 2 June Pants Inner Pocket (mirrored).

Cut 2 June Pants Outer Pocket (mirrored).

Cut 1 June Pants Waistband (on fold).

Elastic Length

Size XS: 24½″ (62.2cm)

Size S: 26½″ (67.3cm)

Size M: 28½″ (72.4cm)

Size L: 31″ (78.7cm)

Size XL: 34″ (86.4cm)

Size XXL: 37″ (94cm)

Construction

Unless otherwise noted, use a ⅜″ (1cm) seam allowance for all seams. For alternatives to finishing seams without a serger, see Finishing Seams (page 51).

ATTACH THE POCKETS

1   Place the inner pocket and front pant leg, right sides together, and pin along the curved edge.

2   Sew the inner pocket to the front pant leg with a ¼″ (6mm) seam allowance, following the curve. *fig. A*

3   Fold the inner pocket over to the inside of the pant leg so it is no longer visible from the front side. Iron to keep in place.

4   From the front side, topstitch the inner pocket ¼″ (6mm) from the edge. *fig. B*

5   With right sides together, place the outer pocket over the inner pocket so the outer pocket lines up with the top and side of the pant leg. Pin in place. *fig. C*

6   Not catching the front pant, sew the pockets together around the curve. Start at the top of the pant; then continue to the side of the pant. Serge the seam allowance. *fig. D*

7   Repeat Steps 1–6 with the other front pant and pockets.

CONSTRUCT THE PANTS

1 Align the two front pants along the crotch seam, right sides together. Pin.

2 Sew the fronts together along the crotch seam. Serge the seam allowance.

3 Repeat Steps 1–2 with the back pant legs. *fig. A*

4 Align the front and back of the pants, right sides together, matching crotch seams. Starting from the center of the crotch and working outward, pin the front and back inner legs of the pants together down to the hem. *figs. B & C*

5 Starting at one hem, sew the front and back pants together at the inner leg, continuing through the crotch, down to the hem of the other pant leg.

6 Line up the outer sides of the front and back. Pin down each leg. Make sure the outer pocket piece is laying flat. Treat the side of the outer pocket as a continuation of the front pant legs.

7 Sew the outer leg seam on both sides. Serge the seam allowances. *fig. D*

8 Turn the pants right side out. Serge the bottom raw hem. Then fold the hem under twice, using the width of the serge hem as the fold guide. Topstitch in place. This creates a narrow hem.

CONSTRUCT THE WAISTBAND

1 Lay waistband pieces right sides together and sew together at the short ends to create a loop.

2 Fold the waistband in half lengthwise, wrong sides together, and press all the way around to create a crease. *figs. A & B*

3 Form the elastic into a loop. Then, making sure it isn't twisted, overlap the ends of ½″ (1.2cm) and sew together. Sew a couple lines to make the attachment sturdy. *fig. C*

4 Unfold the waistband and insert the elastic, making it flush with the crease in the waistband. Make this aligned across a 10″ (25.4cm) section of the waistband. *fig. D*

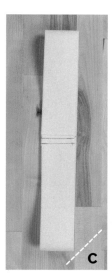

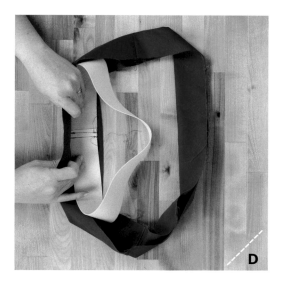

5 Starting at the beginning of the 10″ (25.4cm) section, sew the waistband closed around the elastic, making sure not to catch the elastic with the needle. *fig. E*

As you continue sewing, open the waistband fold, insert the elastic a few inches at a time, and fold the waistband closed around it. Then continue sewing. Eventually, you'll have to pull and scrunch the fabric in order to continue closing it around the elastic. Continue sewing until the waistband is closed around the elastic all the way around. *fig. F*

6 Evenly distribute the scrunched fabric all the way around the elastic. *fig. G*

7 Place the waistband on the sewing machine. Stretch a section so the fabric lays flat on the elastic, and then sew through all layers in the middle of the waistband. Continue around the waistband, constantly stretching as you sew. *fig. H*

8 Repeat Step 7 to add two more lines of stitching. Add one line of stitching above the first line, and another below the first line. *fig. I*

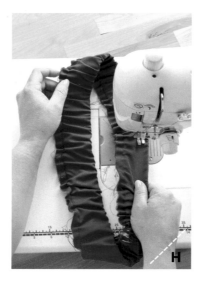

ATTACH THE WAISTBAND

1 Turn the pants inside out. Align one pant side seam with the seam of the waistband, right sides together. Begin sewing the waistband to the pants, stretching the waistband so the bottom raw edge lays flat against the pants. Continue all the way around the waistband and pants. Serge the seam allowance.

Make June Shorts   Making shorts from this pattern is simple—and in fact, it's a great idea when you don't have as much material to work with. Simply measure the desired inseam from the crotch down the leg of the pants. Then, add 1" (2.5cm) to account for the hem. Cut the pattern pieces to this new length.

Avery Tote

HAVE LARGE SECTIONS OF QUILT LEFTOVER FROM A PREVIOUS PROJECT? THE AVERY TOTE IS A GREAT WAY TO UTILIZE THEM WHILE CREATING SOMETHING INCREDIBLY BEAUTIFUL AND EXTREMELY FUNCTIONAL. CREATED TO BE SIMPLE AND CLASSIC IN ITS CLEAN LINES AND MINIMAL STRUCTURE, THIS PROJECT IS A GREAT AND SIMPLE WAY TO START YOUR JOURNEY INTO SEWING WITH UPCYCLED MATERIALS. IT'S ALSO THE PERFECT PROJECT TO EXPERIMENT WITH DIFFERENT DIMENSIONS. AFTER YOU HAVE THE STEPS DOWN TO CREATE THIS TOTE, WE ENCOURAGE YOU TO TRY TO MAKE SMALLER OR LARGER VERSIONS FOR DIFFERENT OCCASIONS. TO SHARE YOUR PROJECT, USE **#averyquiltedtote**

Quilt, blanket, or other vintage textile 30″ × 42″ (76.2cm × 106.7cm) or 2 pieces 15″ × 21″ (38.1 × 53.3cm)

2 yards (1.9m) of 1″ (2.5cm) cotton webbing/ cotton belting trim

40-weight cotton sewing machine thread

30″ piece of extra-wide double-fold ½″ bias tape

4 cones serger thread

TOOLS

Water soluble marker or pencil

Scissors

Sewing machine

Serger

110/18 sewing needle

110/18 serger needles

Iron

Ruler

CUTTING LIST

Cut 2 Avery Tote Main pieces.

Cut 2 cotton webbing strips 30″ (76.2cm).

Construction

Unless otherwise noted, use a ½″ (1.2cm) seam allowance for all seams. As a reminder, for alternatives to finishing seams without a serger, see Finishing Seams (page 51).

ADD STRAPS

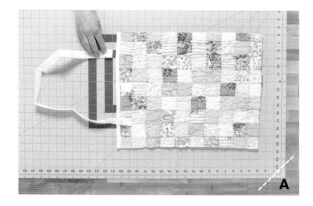

1. Following the instructions in Attaching Bias Tape to an Edge (page 43), bind the top (one 14½″/36.8cm side) of each rectangle, if necessary.

2. On one piece of cotton webbing, fold one edge of the cotton webbing under 1″ (2.5cm) and place it on the right side of one tote piece using the pattern marking. Pin. *fig. A*

3. Sew the webbing to the quilt piece in the shape of a square, catching the section of webbing that is folded under. *fig. B*

Strap attached to tote

4. Sew an *X* through the square for added sturdiness.

5. Repeat Steps 2–4 to attach the other side of the first strap. Make sure you lay out the cotton webbing to ensure the strap is not twisted before sewing.

6. Repeat Steps 2–5 to add the second strap to the other side of the tote bag.

ASSEMBLE TOTE

1 Place the tote pieces right sides together. Pin in place.

2 Sew down each side of the tote. Sew across the bottom of the tote. Leave the top open.

3 Serge the sides and bottom seam allowances of the tote.

CREATE BOX CORNERS

1 Draw a 2″ (5cm) square on both bottom corners. *fig. A*

2 Cut out the marked squares. *fig. B*

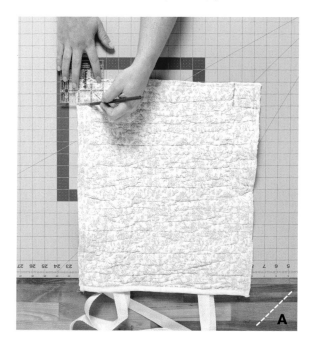

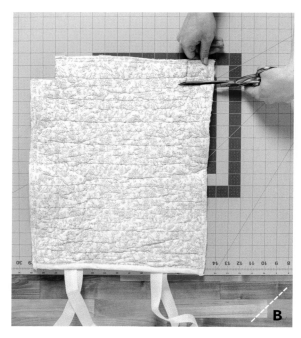

C

3 At the corners of each square, pull the tote apart so the side seam and bottom seam match up. Pin in place. *fig. C*

4 Sew along the cut edge and then serge. *fig. D*

5 Repeat Steps 3–4 for the second corner.

6 Flip the tote right side out, and push out the bottom corners. *fig. E*

D

E

Jet Clutch

THE JET CLUTCH WAS BORN WHEN WE NOTICED THAT WE HAD A GROWING PILE OF QUILT AND FABRIC SCRAPS FILLING UP THE STUDIO—PIECES THAT WERE TOO SMALL FOR CLOTHING BUT TOO BEAUTIFUL TO DISCARD. WE DECIDED THAT THESE BEAUTIFUL SCRAPS NEEDED TO BE SHOWCASED, AND A SMALL CARRYALL BAG WAS THE PERFECT WAY TO ACHIEVE THAT. WHETHER YOU'RE STEPPING OUT FOR A NIGHT ON THE TOWN OR YOU NEED A VERSATILE STORAGE SOLUTION FOR SMALLER ITEMS, THE JET CLUTCH IS THE PERFECT COMPANION FOR ALL YOUR ESSENTIALS. TO SHARE YOUR PROJECT, USE **#jetquiltedclutch**

MATERIALS

Vintage quilt or textile scraps to make up two rectangles 12″ × 8″ (30.5 × 20.3cm)

¼ yard (22.9cm) of non-stretch cotton fabric

30″ (76.2cm) piece of extra-wide double-fold ½″ (1.2cm) bias tape

9″ (22.9cm) zipper

40-weight cotton sewing machine thread

TOOLS

Water soluble marker or pencil

Scissors

Sewing machine

110/18 sewing machine needle

Iron

CUTTING LIST

Cut 2 bias tape strips 6″ (15.2cm) for zipper tabs.

Cut 1 bias tape strip 16″ (40.6cm).

Cut 2 Jet Clutch pieces from main fabric.

Cut 2 Jet Clutch pieces from cotton fabric.

NOTE

If you prefer, you can just measure the dimensions for the clutch piece. It's a rectangle 12″ × 8″ (30.5 × 20.3cm).

Construction

Unless otherwise noted, use a ½″ (1.2cm) seam allowance for all seams. As a reminder, for alternatives to finishing seams without a serger, see Finishing Seams (page 51).

PREPARE THE ZIPPER

1 Unfold the two pieces of 6″ (15.2cm) of bias tape and press flat.

2 Fold the zipper tabs in half to create two pieces 1″ × 3″ (2.5 × 7.6cm). Press. *fig. A*

3 Line up the zipper tabs against both ends of the zipper so the fold is almost touching the beginning and end of the zipper. Pin. *fig. B*

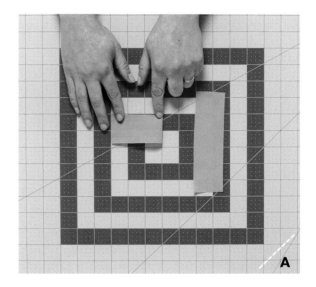

4 Sew across both zipper tabs, attaching them to the zipper as close to the edge of the tabs and with the smallest seam allowance possible. *fig. C*

5 Trim the zipper tab ends so the total length of the zipper and tabs is 12″ (30.5cm).

ATTACHING THE ZIPPER

1 Lay the zipper, facing down, across the top of the right side of one quilt clutch piece (the 12″/30.5cm side). *fig.A*

2 Lay the lining piece on top of the zipper so it lines up with the quilt piece underneath. *fig.B*

3 Sew the three layers together across the top, as close to the zipper teeth as your machine will allow. If you have a zipper foot, you're welcome to use it, but it isn't necessary. *fig.C*

4 Pull the lining and quilt open, and press each side down and away from the zipper with the iron.

5 Topstitch along both sides of the zipper, making sure the lining doesn't bunch underneath. If bunching happens, the zipper will catch on the fabric while being opened and closed. *fig.D*

6 Repeat Steps 1–5 with the other lining and quilt pieces.

ASSEMBLE THE CLUTCH

Keep the zipper in the open position while assembling.

1 Match up the quilt pieces and the lining pieces, right sides together, so the zipper is in the center. *fig.A*

2 Topstitch the open edge of the 16″ (40.6cm) piece of bias tape so it remains closed. This will be the clutch strap.

3 Insert the clutch strap in between the quilt pieces, 2″ (5cm) down from the zipper, so the loop is on the inside. Pin in place. *fig.B*

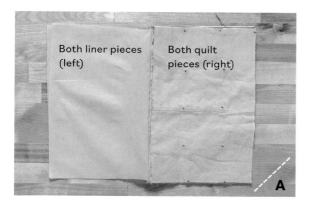

4 Pin around the whole project, securing the two layers together on each side. Mark a 4″ (10.2cm) gap at the bottom center of the lining pieces.

5 Starting at one mark on the lining, sew all the way around the project, leaving the 4″ (10.2cm) gap open. Backstitch at the beginning and end. *fig.C*

6 Trim the corners of the quilt pieces, making sure not to cut through the stitches. *fig.D*

7 Remove the pins.

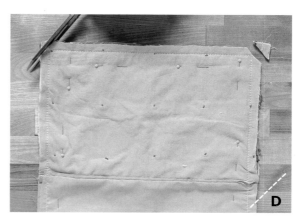

FINISH THE CLUTCH

1 Reach a hand inside the unsewn space on the lining, and pull the clutch right side out. *fig. A*

2 Use your fingers or a pencil to push out the corners of the clutch.

3 Pull the lining out so it lays flush outside the bag, and fold the unsewn seam inward to enclose the raw edges.

4 Sew the fold in place, as close to the edge as possible. *fig. B*

5 Push the lining back into the clutch and push the corners into place.

A

B

Balaclava

JUST LIKE THE POLISH AND PRUSSIAN SOLDIERS FROM THE 19TH CENTURY, YOU, TOO, CAN BATTLE THE COLD IN STYLE WITH A QUILTED BALACLAVA. LIVING UP HERE IN VERMONT, WE KNEW WE NEEDED TO CREATE AN OUTERWEAR ACCESSORY THAT WOULD KEEP US WARM THROUGH THE BRUTAL WINTERS. LUCKILY, QUILTS ARE MEANT TO KEEP YOU WARM, AND WHEN YOU ADD A BIT OF SHERPA FABRIC TO THE MIX, THERE IS NOTHING TOASTIER. THE QUILTED BALACLAVA IS ONE-SIZE-FITS-ALL WITH ADJUSTABLE FLAPS IN THE FRONT THAT PROTECT YOUR FACE FROM THE COLDEST OF WEATHER. TO SHARE YOUR PROJECT, USE

#quiltedbalaclava

MATERIALS

Vintage quilt or textile scraps to make up two rectangles 18″ × 15″ (45.7 × 38.1cm)

Shearling or sherpa to make two rectangles 12½″ × 14″ (31.8 × 35.6cm)

Six sets of ¾″ (1.9cm) metal snaps

40-weight cotton-weight sewing machine thread

TOOLS

Water soluble marker or pencil

Scissors

Sewing machine

110/18 needle

Iron

Snap pliers

CUTTING LIST

Cut 2 Balaclava Hood from main fabric (mirrored).

Cut 2 Balaclava Flap A from main fabric.

Cut 2 Balaclava Flap B from main fabric.

Cut 2 Balaclava Hood from shearling or sherpa (mirrored).

Construction

Unless otherwise noted, use a ⅜″ (1cm) seam allowance for all seams. As a reminder, for alternatives to finishing seams without a serger, see Finishing Seams (page 51). Note that for this project, you need two top snaps and six bottom snaps. So, while you will likely only be able to purchase snaps in sets, if you already have snaps, you only need two top posts. Transfer all pattern marks onto the cut fabric pieces.

PREPARE THE BALACLAVA PIECES

1 Using the pattern, mark the snap placements on the right sides of two balaclava flap pieces. One piece should have two marks for the top posts. The other piece should have six marks for the bottom posts. *fig. A*

2 Lay out the quilt hood pieces, right side up. Grab the one that has the curved edge on the left side and the flap with the top snap markings (top snap markings should be furthest from the seam line). With right sides together, place the flap on the hood piece, aligning the edges. Sew together. *fig. B*

3 Repeat Step 2 with the second quilt hood piece and the quilt flap that has the bottom snap markings.

4 With right sides together, place one of the remaining balaclava quilt flaps on the bottom straight side of the shearling hood piece and sew it together.

5 Repeat with the final quilt flap and remaining shearling hood piece.

6 Align the quilted hood pieces, right sides together, and sew from top to bottom along the curved side. *fig. C*

7 Align the shearling hood pieces, right sides together, and sew from top to bottom along the curved side.

A

B

C

ASSEMBLE THE BALACLAVA

1 With the right sides together, insert the quilted hood into the shearling hood so the center seams match up. Pin. *fig. A*

2 Sew around the perimeter of the balaclava, including the flaps, and leaving approximately 4″–5″ (10.2cm–12.7cm) open and unsewn at the center bottom of the balaclava. *fig. B*

3 Trim flap corners, making sure not to cut into the stitches. *fig. C*

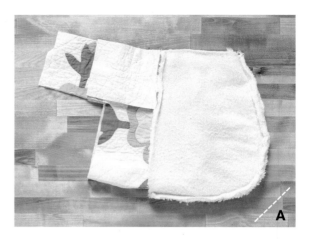

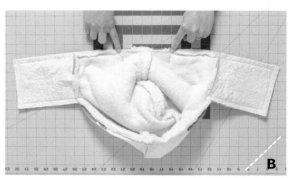

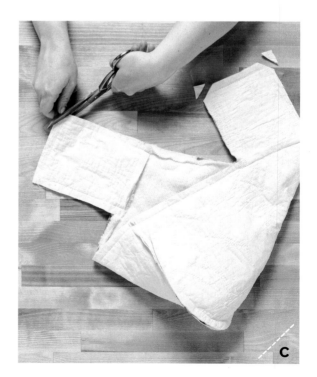

FINISH THE BALACLAVA

1 Pull the balaclava right side out through the hole at the center bottom. *fig. A*

2 Use a pencil to push out the corners of the flaps.

3 Fold the opening at the bottom of the balaclava inward, hiding the raw edges.

4 Topstitch around the entire perimeter of the balaclava, closing the opening at the bottom. *fig. B*

5 Attach the snaps, adding two top posts and six bottom posts to the marked spots, following the instructions in Attaching Snaps (page 47). *fig. C*

Holly Stocking

WHEN WE THINK OF THE HOLIDAYS, WE THINK OF COZINESS, GATHERING WITH FRIENDS AND FAMILY, AND TRADITIONS—AND THE HOLLY STOCKING FITS RIGHT IN. THIS PROJECT IS A WONDERFUL GIFT IDEA FOR ALL YOUR LOVED ONES, MADE EVEN MORE SPECIAL BY INCORPORATING QUILTS AND TEXTILES THAT WERE MADE BY PAST GENERATIONS OR THAT HOLD SPECIAL MEANING WITHIN YOUR FAMILY OR INNER CIRCLE. TO SHARE YOUR PROJECT, USE **#hollyquiltedstocking**

MATERIALS

Vintage quilt or textile scraps to make up two rectangles 19″ × 13″ (48.3 × 33cm)

Shearling or sherpa fabric to make up two rectangles 5″ × 9″ (12.7 × 22.9cm)

40-weight cotton sewing machine thread

4x overlock thread

6½″ (16.5cm)-long strip of extra-wide double-fold ½″ (1.2cm) bias tape

TOOLS

Sewing machine

Serger

110/18 sewing machine needle

110/18 serger needles

CUTTING LIST

Cut 2 Holly Stocking Main from main fabric (mirrored).

Cut 2 Holly Stocking Cuff from shearling or sherpa.

Construction

Unless otherwise noted, use a ½″ (1.2cm) seam allowance for all seams. As a reminder, for alternatives to finishing seams without a serger, see Finishing Seams (page 51).

PREPARE THE STOCKING PIECES

1 Serge across one 9″ (22.9cm) edge of each shearling rectangle.

2 Fold the serged shearling seams under (wrong sides together) by 1″ (2.5cm) and sew through the serged line to keep it in place. *fig. A*

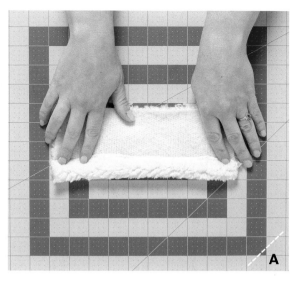

3 Align one shearling rectangle with the top of one quilt stocking piece, right sides together. Sew the shearling piece to the top of the quilt stocking piece. Repeat for the second stocking piece. *fig. B*

> **NOTE**
>
> It is generally easier to move the project through the sewing machine with the quilt piece on top and the shearling or sherpa piece on the bottom.

4 Fold the shearling rectangles over to the right sides of the stocking pieces. Pin. *fig. C*

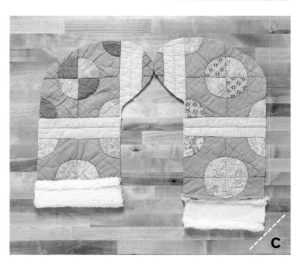

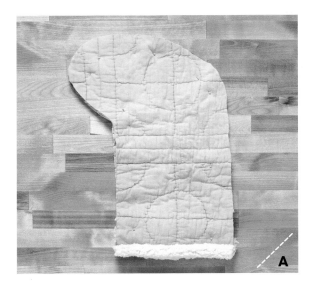

ASSEMBLE THE STOCKING

1 Align the quilted stocking pieces (with shearling still folded over) right sides together. Pin. *fig. A*

2 Fold the bias tape strip in half so it creates a loop.

3 Insert the looped bias tape 3″ (7.6cm) from the top of the stocking, between the two layers and on the opposite side of the stocking's foot. Pin. *fig. B*

4 Sew around the entire stocking, leaving the top open and attaching the loop. *fig. C*

5 Serge the seam allowance.

6 Pull the stocking right side out. *fig. D*

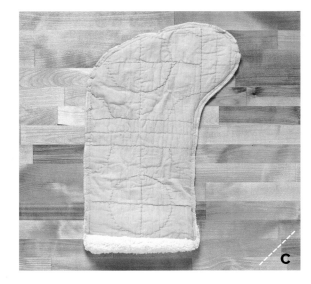

ABOUT THE AUTHORS

Meet the passionate minds behind Kitty Badhands: Kat and Dale, a dynamic husband-and-wife team based in the picturesque town of Burlington, Vermont. Their love for textiles and commitment to the environment drives their family-owned and -operated business.

Kitty Badhands started with a spark ignited by Kathleen McVeigh's admiration for repurposing quilts and vintage textiles. Over time, that spark grew into a slow-fashion clothing brand that embraces both style and sustainability. Our designs embody modern silhouettes while carrying a sense of nostalgia, resulting in timeless pieces that empower you to feel confident and chic.

In a world that often moves too fast, our aim in sharing this book with you is twofold: to inspire you to craft a fabulous wardrobe that you will wear for years to come and to celebrate all the talented sewists, artists, quilters, and makers of the past. Let's draw from their artistry, honoring the rich history of craft while also considering the kind of planet that we hope to leave for the future sewists, artists, quilters, and makers to live (and create) on.

Previous Kitty Badhands work